The Virgin Of The World

Hermes

Kessinger Publishing's Rare Reprints

Thousands of Scarce and Hard-to-Find Books on These and other Subjects!

- Americana
- Ancient Mysteries
- Animals
- Anthropology
- Architecture
- Arts
- Astrology
- Bibliographies
- Biographies & Memoirs
- Body, Mind & Spirit
- Business & Investing
- Children & Young Adult
- Collectibles
- Comparative Religions
- Crafts & Hobbies
- Earth Sciences
- Education
- Ephemera
- Fiction
- Folklore
- Geography
- Health & Diet
- History
- Hobbies & Leisure
- Humor
- Illustrated Books
- Language & Culture
- Law
- Life Sciences
- Literature
- Medicine & Pharmacy
- Metaphysical
- Music
- Mystery & Crime
- Mythology
- Natural History
- Outdoor & Nature
- Philosophy
- Poetry
- Political Science
- Science
- Psychiatry & Psychology
- Reference
- Religion & Spiritualism
- Rhetoric
- Sacred Books
- Science Fiction
- Science & Technology
- Self-Help
- Social Sciences
- Symbolism
- Theatre & Drama
- Theology
- Travel & Explorations
- War & Military
- Women
- Yoga
- *Plus Much More!*

**We kindly invite you to view our catalog list at:
http://www.kessinger.net**

THIS ARTICLE WAS EXTRACTED FROM THE BOOK:

Virgin of the World of Hermes Mercurius Trismegistus

BY THIS AUTHOR:

Hermes

ISBN 1564596729

READ MORE ABOUT THE BOOK AT OUR WEB SITE:

http://www.kessinger.net

OR ORDER THE COMPLETE
BOOK FROM YOUR FAVORITE STORE

ISBN 1564596729

The Virgin of the World.

Hermes.

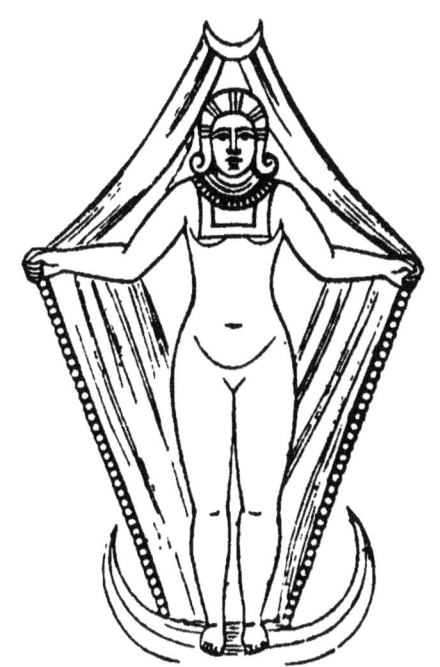

"I, Isis, am everything that has been, and that is, and that shall be, and no mortal hath lifted my veil."
(In this Treatise, the Goddess is represented as herself lifting her veil.)

THE VIRGIN OF THE WORLD.

I.

*   *   *   *

HAVING thus spoken, Isis first pours out for Horos the sweet draught of immortality which souls receive from the Gods, and thus begins the most holy discourse.

Heaven, crowned with stars, is placed above universal nature, O my son Horos, and nothing is wanting to it of that which constitutes the whole world. It is necessary, then, that all nature should be adorned and completed by that which is above her, for this Order could not proceed from below to above. The supremacy

[of

of the greater mysteries over the lesser is imperative. Celestial order reigns over terrestrial order, as being absolutely determined, and inaccessible to the idea of death. Wherefore, the things below lament, being filled with fear before the marvellous beauty and eternal permanence of the heavenly world. For, indeed, a spectacle worthy of contemplation and desire were these magnificences of heaven, revelations of the God as yet unknown, and this sumptuous majesty of night illumined with a penetrating radiance, albeit less than that of the sun, and all these other mysteries which move above in harmonious cadence, ruling and maintaining the things below by secret influences. And so long as the Universal Architect refrained from putting an end to this incessant fear, to these anxious investigations, ignorance enveloped the universe. But when He judged good to reveal Himself to the world, He breathed into the Gods the enthusiasm of love, and poured into their mind the splendour which His bosom contained, that they might first be inspired with the will to seek, next with the desire to find, and lastly with the power to readjust.

Now, my wondrous child Horos, all this could not happen among mortals, for as yet they did not exist; but it took place in the universal Soul in sympathy with the mysteries of heaven. This was Hermes, the Kosmic Thought. He beheld the universe of things, and having seen, he understood, and having understood, he had the power to manifest and to reveal. That which he thought, he wrote; that which he wrote, he in great part concealed, wisely silent and speaking by turns, so that while the world should last, these things might be sought. And thus, having enjoined upon the Gods, his brethren, that they should follow in his train, he ascended to the

[stars.

(3)

stars. But he had for successor his son, and the heir of his knowledges, Tat, and a little later, Asclepios, son of Imouthè, by the counsels of Pan and Hephaistos,* and all those for whom sovereign Providence reserved an exact knowledge of heavenly things.

Hermes then justified himself in the presence of those who surrounded him, in that he had not delivered the integral theory to his son, on account of his youth. But I, having arisen, beheld with mine eyes, which see the invisible secrets of the beginnings of things,† and at length, but with certainty, I understood that the sacred symbols of the Kosmic elements were hidden near the secrets of Osiris. Hermes returned to heaven, having pronounced an invocatory speech.

It is not fitting, O my Son, that this recital be left incomplete; thou must be informed of the words of

---

* The text of this passage presents great difficulties and uncertainties. The words in Canter's edition, Ἀσκληπιὸς ὁ ἱμούθης σπανὸς και 'ηφαίστου ἑουλαῖς, Canter reads Asclepios, Ammon, and Hephaistobulus. Patrizzi changes 'ηφαίστου ἑουλαῖς into 'ηφαιστοἑούλης, and renders it Asclepios Imuthes, Spanos and Hephæstobulus. Others read πανός in place of σπανός, which is plausible enough, but at the same time they preserve 'ηφαιστοἑούλης, and then ἱμούθης becomes a surname of Asclepios, who would thus be son of Pan and Hephaistoboulè, an absolutely unknown goddess. But in another fragment we read, a little further on, Ἀσκληπιὸς ὁ ἱμούθης and Ἀσκληπιὸς ὁ ἡφαίστου, and the word πάλιν indicates that it refers to the same Asclepios, and not to two persons of the same name. It may be, then, that Imouthè was the name of his mother, as Fabricius supposes. Is it not likely that it is the Greek form of "Mouth"? The Egyptian Asclepios was represented bald, according to Synésios; the word σπανός, which means bald, might then be retained. But in this case, in order that the phrase may have a meaning, it would be necessary to change ἑουλαῖς into ἑουλαῖος, and translate:—Asclepios, the bald Imouthès, and counsellor of Hephaistos.

† This sentence is very obscure; the participles are in the masculine, as though the author had forgotten that a goddess was speaking. I believe the text of the passage must have been altered.

[Hermes

Hermes when he laid down his books. "O sacred books," he said, "of the Immortals, ye in whose pages my hand has recorded the remedies by which incorruptibility is conferred, remain for ever beyond the reach of destruction and of decay, invisible and concealed from all who frequent these regions, until the day shall come in which the ancient heaven shall bring forth instruments worthy of you, whom the Creator shall call souls."

Having pronounced upon his books this invocation, he wrapped them in their coverings, returned into the sphere which belonged to him, and all remained hidden for a sufficient space.

And Nature, O my Son, was barren until the hour in which those who are ordained to survey the heavens, advancing towards God, the King of all things, deplored the general inertia, and affirmed the necessity of setting forth the universe. No other than Himself could accomplish this work.

"We pray Thee," said they, "to consider that which already is, and that which is necessary for the future."

At these words, the God smiled benignant, and commanded Nature to exist. And, issuing with His voice, the FEMININE came forth in her perfect beauty. The Gods with amaze beheld this marvel. And the great Ancestor, pouring out for Nature an elixir, commanded her to be fruitful; and forthwith, penetrating the universe with His glance, He cried, "Let heaven be the plenitude of all things, and of the air, and of the ether." God spake, and it was done. But Nature, communing with herself, understood that she might not transgress the commandment of the Father, and, uniting herself to Labour, she produced a most beautiful daughter, whom she called Invention, and to whom God accorded being.

And having differentiated created forms, He filled
[them

them with mysteries, and gave the command of them to Invention.

Then, not willing that the upper world should be inactive, He saw fit to fill it with spirits, in order that no region should remain in immobility and inertia; and in the accomplishment of His work He used His sacred art. For, taking of Himself such essence as was necessary, and mingling with it an intellectual flame, He combined with these other materials by unknown ways. And having achieved by secret formulas the union of these principles, He endowed with motion the universal combination. Gradually, in the midst of the protoplasm, glittered a substance more subtle, purer, more limpid, than the elements from which it was generated. It was transparent, and the Artist alone perceived it. Soon, it attained its perfection, being neither melted by the fire, nor chilled by the breath, but possessing the stability of a special combination, and having its proper type and constitution. He bestowed on it a happy name, and, according to the similitude of its energies, He called it Self-Consciousness.

Of this product he formed myriads of Souls, employing the choicest part of the mixture for the end which He had in view, proceeding with order and measure, according to His knowledge and His reason. The souls were not necessarily different, but the choicest part, animated by the Divine motion, was not identical with the rest. The first layer was superior to the second, more perfect and pure; the second, inferior truly to the first, was superior to the third; and thus, until sixty degrees, was completed the total number. Only, God established this law, that all equally should be eternal, being of one essence, whose forms He alone determines.

He traced the limits of their sojourn on the heights
[of

of nature, so that they might turn the wheel according to the laws of Order and of wise discretion, for the joy of their Father.

Then, having summoned to these splendid regions of ether the souls of every grade, He said to them: "O souls, beautiful children of my breath and of my care, you whom I have produced with my hands, in order to consecrate you to my universe, hear my words as a law:—Quit not the place assigned to you by my will. The abode which awaits you is heaven, with its galaxy of stars and its thrones of virtue. If you attempt any transgression against my decree, I swear by my sacred breath, by that elixir of which I formed you, and by my creative hands, that I will speedily forge for you chains and cast you into punishment."

Having thus spoken, God, my Master, mingled together the rest of the congenial elements, earth and water, and pronouncing certain powerful and mystic words—albeit different from the first—He breathed into the liquid protoplasm motion and life, rendered it thicker and more plastic, and formed of it living beings of human shape. That which remained He gave to the loftiest souls inhabiting the region of the Gods in the neighbourhood of the stars, who are called the Sacred Genii. "Work," said He, "my children, offspring of my nature; take the residue of my task, and let each one of you make beings in his image. I will give you models."

Therewith He took the Zodiac and ordained the world in conformity with vital movements, placing the animal signs after those of human form. And after having given forth the creative forces and generative breath for the whole range of beings yet to come, He

[withdrew.

withdrew, promising to unite to every visible work an invisible breath and a reproductive principle, so that each being might engender its similar without necessity to create continually new entities.*

And what did the souls do, O my Mother?

And Isis answered:—They took the mingled material, O my Son Horos, and began to reflect thereon, and to adore this combination, the work of the Father. Next, they sought to discover of what it was composed, which, indeed, it was not easy to find. Then, fearing

---

* This recital of the creation of the souls recalls the *Timæus* of Plato. After all the Gods were born, the Artificer of the universe thus addressed them:—" Gods of gods, of whom I am the Creator and Father, and who, formed by me, are by my will indissoluble, learn what I now say to you. . . . In order that mortal natures may exist, and that the universe may be indeed universal, turn yourselves according to your nature to the formation of animals, imitating the power which I employed in the generation of yourselves. . . . I myself will deliver the seeds and beginnings; and for the rest do you weave together the mortal and immortal nature, constructing and producing animals." He said, and into the same cup in which He had mingled and tempered the soul of the universe, He poured the residue, and mixed it in the same manner, but in less pure combinations of a second and third order. And having constituted the universe, He allotted souls to the stars in equal number, distributing each to each; and causing every one to mount his vehicle, He displayed to them the nature of the universe, and taught them the laws of Destiny.

[It may be added, also, that this legend, quaint and grotesque as it is in many of its details, is, likewise, in accord with the Kabbala, which recounts the pre-mundane history of the souls, their creation, their transgression, and their punishment, in much the same fashion. The creation of the visible world by the " working gods," or Titans, as agents for the Supreme God, is a thoroughly Hermetic idea, recognizable in all religious systems, and in accord with modern scientific research, which shews us everywhere the Divine Power operating secretly through natural forces.

A. K.]

[that

that this search might excite the anger of the Father, they set themselves to carry out His commands. Therefore, taking the upper portion of the protoplasm, that which was lightest, they created of it the race of birds. The compound having now become more compact and assuming a denser consistency, they formed of it the quadrupeds; while of the thickest part which needed a moist vehicle for its support, they made fishes. The remainder, being cold and heavy, was employed by the souls in the creation of reptiles.

Forthwith, O my Son, proud of their work, they were not afraid to transgress the Divine law, and, in spite of the prohibition, they receded from their appointed limits. Not willing to remain longer in the same abode, they moved ceaselessly, and repose seemed to them death.*

But, O my Son—(thus Hermes informed me)—their conduct could not escape the eye of the Lord God of all things; He minded to punish them, and to prepare for them hard bonds. The Ruler and Master of the universe resolved then for the penance of the souls, to mould the human organism, and having called me to

---

* In reading this allegory, it must be borne in mind that the word "Soul" is used as a general term for all Egos or Intelligences, whether Genii or Men. Further, that in these Fragments, as in the Hebrew Scriptures, the same truths are repeated under different symbols in different passages. Hence the creation of Nature and of "differentiated forms" has already been otherwise depicted in a previous paragraph; and the whole process of the evolution of the Soul has been epitomized in the fable of the making of the protoplasm. The descent into generation occurs, actually, when the Titans first begin the manipulation of this protoplasm. The human body, although last in manifestation, is really the first in the Divine intention, and is the ultimate cause of all the series of objective forms. Hermetically speaking, there is nothing in the whole universe, save Man.

A. K.

[Him

Him, said Hermes, He spoke in this wise:—"O soul of my soul, holy thought of my thought, how long shall earthly Nature remain sad? How long shall the creation already produced continue inactive and without praise? Bring hither before me all the Gods of heaven."

Thus God spake, quoth Hermes, and all obeyed His decree. "Look upon the earth," He said to them, "and upon all things beneath."

Straightway they looked, and understood the will of the Lord. And when He spoke to them of the creation of Man, asking of each what he could bestow upon the race about to be born, the Sun first replied:—"I will illumine mankind." Then the Moon promised enlightenment in her turn, adding that already she had created Fear, Silence, Sleep, and Memory. Kronos announced that he had begotten Justice and Necessity. Zeus said, "In order to spare the future race perpetual wars, I have generated Fortune, Hope, and Peace." Ares declared himself already father of Conflict, impetuous Zeal, and Emulation. Aphrodite did not wait to be called upon: "As for me, O Master," she said, "I will bestow upon mankind Desire, with voluptuous Joy and Laughter, that the penalty to which our sister Souls are destined may not weigh on them too hardly." These words of Aphrodite, O my Son, were welcomed gladly. "And I," said Hermes, "will endow human nature with Wisdom, Temperance, Persuasion, and Truth; nor will I cease to ally myself with Invention. I will ever protect the mortal life of such men as are born under my signs, seeing that to me the Creator and Father has attributed in the Zodiac, signs of Knowledge and Intelligence; above all, when the movement which draws thereto the stars is in harmony with the physical forces of each." *

He Who is Master of the world rejoiced at hearing these things, and decreed the production of the human race. As for me—said Hermes—I sought what material ought to be employed in the work, and invoked the Lord. He commanded the Souls to give up the residue of the protoplastic substance, which having taken, I found it entirely dried up. Therefore, I used a great excess of water wherewith to renew the combination of the substance, in such wise that the product might be resolvable, yielding, and feeble, and that Force should not be added therein to Intelligence. When I had achieved my work it was beautiful, and I rejoiced in seeing it. And from below I called upon the Lord to behold what I had done. He saw it, and approved. Straightway He ordained that the Souls should be incorporated; and they were seized wth horror on learning what should be their condemnation.

These words, said Isis, struck me. Hearken, my son Horos, for I teach thee a mystery. Our ancestor Kamephes had it also from Hermes, who inscribes the recital of all things; I, in turn, received it from the ancient Kamephes when he admitted me to the initiation of the black veil;† and thou, likewise, O marvellous and illustrious child, receive it from me.

* Heeren sees in these metaphors an allusion to the creation of Pandora in Hesiod. They recall also a passage in the Pymander, wherein the Rulers of the Seven Planets cause Man to participate in their nature; an idea developed likewise by Macrobius in his commentary on the Dream of Scipio.—*Lib. L., chap. xii.*

† Canter translates this by *atramentum*, which would signify initiation by writing; but it is possible that the heads of the initiated persons were covered with a black veil, or perhaps the veil of Isis is here intended.

[The

The Souls were about to be imprisoned in bodies, whereat some sighed and lamented, as when some wild and free animal suddenly enchained, in the first moment of subjection to hard servitude and of severance from the beloved habits of the wilderness, struggles and revolts, refusing to follow its conqueror, and if occasion presents itself, slaying him. Others, again, hissed like serpents, or gave vent to piercing cries and sorrowful words, glancing aimlessly from height to depth.

"Great Heaven," said one, "principle of our birth, ether, pure airs, hands, and sacred breath of the sovereign God, and you, shining Stars, eyes of the Gods, unwearying light of Sun and Moon, our early brethren, what grief, what rending is this! Must we quit these vast, effulgent spaces, this sacred sphere, all these splendors of the empyrean and of the happy republic of the Gods, to be precipitated into these vile and miserable abodes? What crime, O wretched ones, have we committed? How can we have merited, poor sinners that we are, the penalties which await us? Behold the sad future in store for us—to minister to the wants of a fluctuating and dissoluble body! No more may our eyes distinguish the souls divine! Hardly through these watery spheres shall we perceive, with sighs, our ancestral heaven; at intervals even we shall cease altogether to behold it. By this disastrous sentence direct vision is denied to us; we can see only by the aid of the outer light; these are but windows that we possess—not eyes. Nor will our pain be less when we hear in the air the fraternal breathing of the winds with which no longer can we mingle our own, since that will have for its dwelling, instead of the sublime and open world, the narrow prison of the breast! But Thou, Who drivest us forth, and causest us from so

[high

high a seat to descend so low, assign a limit to our sufferings! O Master and Father, so quickly become indifferent to Thy handiwork, appoint a term to our penance, deign to bestow on us some last words, while yet we are able to behold the expanse of the luminous spheres!"

This prayer of the Souls was granted, my son Horos, for the Lord was present; and sitting upon the throne of Truth, thus He addressed them:—

"O Souls; you shall be governed by Desire and Necessity; after me, these shall be your masters and your guides. Souls, subjected to my sceptre which never fails, know that inasmuch as you remain stainless you shall inhabit the regions of the skies. If among you any be found to merit reproach, they shall inhabit abodes destined to them in mortal organisms. If your faults be light, you shall, delivered from the bond of the flesh, return to heaven. But if you become guilty of graver crime, if you turn away from the end for which you have been formed, then indeed you shall dwell neither in heaven nor in human bodies, but thenceforth you shall pass into those of animals without reason." *

---

* It has been questioned whether Hermetic doctrine affirms the Hindu theory of transmigration, to wit—the possibility of the passage of the guilty Ego into lower forms than that of man. We must, I hold, admit the orthodoxy of the doctrine, which, when rightly understood, involves no paradox. In the Divine Pymander, it is clearly set forth that if a human soul continue evil "it shall neither taste of immortality nor be partaker of the good, but being drawn back it returneth into creeping things; and this is the condemnation of an evil soul." Yet, Trismegistus hastens immediately to explain and qualify this statement by adding that such a calamity cannot befall any truly human soul—that is, a soul possessing the divine Mind, however fallen from grace, for so long as the soul retains this living fire

Having thus spoken, O my son Horos, He breathed upon them, and said, "It is not according to chance that I have ordained your destiny; if you act ill, it will be worse; it will be better if your actions are worthy of your birth. It is myself and not another who will be your witness and your judge. Understand that it is because of your past errors that you are to be punished and shut up in fleshly bodies. In different bodies, as I have already told you, your re-births will be different. Dissolution shall be a benefit, restoring your former happy condition. But if your conduct be unworthy of me, your prudence, becoming blinded and guiding you backwards, will cause you to take for good fortune that which is really a chastisement, and to dread a happier lot as though it were a cruel injury. The most just among you shall, in their future transformations, approximate to the

---

it is the soul of a man, and man "is not to be compared to any brute beast upon the earth, but to them that are above in heaven, that are called Gods." But there is a condition so low and lost that at length the divine flame is quenched, and the soul is left dark and Godless, a human soul no longer. "And such a soul, O Son," says Hermes, "hath no Mind; *wherefore neither must such an one be called Man.*" Therefore, while it is true that "no other body is capable of a human soul, neither is it lawful for a man's soul to fall into the body of an unreasonable living thing," so also is it true that a soul, bereft of its Divine Particle which alone made it human, is human no longer, and, following the universal law of affinity, straightway gravitates to its proper level, sinking to its similars, and drawn to its analogues. Nevertheless, when its purgation is accomplished, such a soul may "come to itself and say, I will arise and go unto my Father."

There are some Rabbis indeed who have thought such an occult significance to lie hid in the parable of the prodigal; swine being accounted universally a figure of lust and sordid desire. The Hermetic doctrine, thus interpreted, is identical with that of the Kabbala on the same point, as we shall elsewhere have occasion to shew; and also with the teaching of Apollonius of Tyana.—(*v. Perfect Way*, III., 21, etc.)

A. K.

[divine

divine, becoming among men, upright kings, true philosophers, leaders and legislators, true seers, collectors of salutary plants, cunning musicians, intelligent astronomers, wise augurs, instructed ministrants all beautiful and good offices; as among birds are the eagles which pursue not nor devour those of their own kind, and do not permit weaker ones to be attacked in their presence, because justice is in the nature of the eagle; among quadrupeds, the lion, for he is a strong animal, untamed by slumber, in a mortal body performing immortal toils, and by nothing tired nor beguiled; among reptiles, the dragon, because he is powerful, living long, innocent, and a friend of men, allowing himself to be tamed, having no venom, and leaving old age, approximating to the nature of the Gods; among fishes, the dolphin, for this creature, taking pity on those who fall into the sea, will carry them to land if they still live, and will abstain from devouring them if dead, although it is the most voracious of all aquatic animals."

Having spoken these words, God became an Incorruptible Intelligence (*i.e.*, resumed the unmanifest).

After these things, my son Horos, there arose out of the earth an exceeding powerful Spirit, unencumbered with any corporeal envelope, strong in wisdom, but savage and fearful; although he could not be ignorant of the knowledge he sought, seeing the type of the human body to be beautiful and august of aspect, and perceiving that the souls were about to enter into their envelopes:—

"What are these," said he, "O Hermes, Secretary of the Gods?" "These are men," replied Hermes. "It is a rash work," said he, "to make man with such penetrating eyes, such a subtle tongue, such a delicate

[hearing

hearing that can hear even those things which concern him not, such a fine scent, and in his hands a sense of touch capable of appropriating everything. O generating Spirit, thinkest thou it is well that he should be free from care—this future investigator of the fine mysteries of Nature? Wilt thou leave him exempt from suffering—he whose thought will search out the limits of the earth? Mankind will dig up the roots of plants, they will study the properties of natural juices, they will observe the nature of stones, they will dissect not only animals but themselves, desiring to know how they have been formed. They will stretch forth their daring hands over the sea, and, cutting down the timber of the wild forest, they will pass from shore to shore seeking one another. They will pursue the inmost secrets of Nature even into the heights, and will study the motions of heaven. Nor is this enough; when nothing yet remains to be known than the furthest boundary of the earth, they will seek even there the last extremities of night. If they apprehend no obstacle, if they live exempt from trouble, beyond reach of any fear or of any anxiety, even heaven itself will not arrest their audacity; they will seek to extend their power over the elements. Teach them, then, desire and hope, in such wise that they may know likewise the dread of accident and of difficulty, and the painful sting of expectation deceived. Let the curiosity of their souls have for balance, desire and fear, care and vain hope. Let their souls be a prey to mutual love, to aspirations and varied longings, now satisfied, now deceived, so that even the sweetness of success may be an allurement to draw them towards misfortune. Let the weight of fevers oppress them, and break in them all desire."

Thou sufferest, Horos, in hearing this thy mother's
[recital?

recital? Surprise and wonder seize thee in presence of the evils which now fall upon poor humanity? That which thou art about to hear is still more sad. The speech of Momos pleased Hermes; he deemed his advice good, and he followed it.

"O, Momos," said he, "the nature of the divine breath which enwraps all things shall not be ineffectual! The Master of the universe has charged me to be His agent and overseer. The Deity of the penetrating eye (Adrastia)* will observe and direct all events; and for my part, I will design a mysterious instrument, a measure inflexible and inviolable, to which everything shall be subject from birth even to final destruction, and which shall be the bond of created entities. This instrument shall rule that which is on the earth, and all the rest."

It is thus—quoth Hermes—that I spoke to Momos; and forthwith the instrument operated. Straightway the souls were incorporated, and I was praised for my work.

Then the Lord summoned anew the assembly of the Gods. They gathered together, and He thus addressed them:—

"Gods, who have received a sovereign and imperishable nature, and the sway of the vast eternity, ye whose office it is to maintain unceasingly the mutual harmony of things, how long shall we govern an empire unknown? How long shall creation remain invisible to the sun and moon? Let each of

* This name appears to have been a marginal interpolation, inserted into the text by a copyist. It serves as a key to what follows, Adrastia (or Nemesis) being the personification of the necessary law (or inflexible instrument) of which Hermes is about to speak.

[us

us undertake his part in the universe. By the exercise of our power let us put an end to the cohesion of inertia. Let chaos become a fable, incredible to posterity. Inaugurate your great labours; I will direct you."

He said, and immediately the Kosmic unity, until now obscure, was opened, and in the heights appeared the heavens with all their mysteries. The earth, hitherto unstable, grew more solid beneath the brightness of the sun, and stood forth adorned with enfolding riches. All things are beautiful in the eyes of God, even that which to mortals appears uncomely, because all is made according to the divine laws. And God rejoiced in beholding His works filled with movement; and with outstretched hands grasping the treasures of nature. "Take these," He said, " O sacred earth, take these, O venerable one, who art to be the mother of all things, and henceforth let nothing be lacking to thee!"

With these words, opening His divine hands, He poured His treasures into the universal font. But yet they were unknown, for the souls newly embodied and unable to support their opprobrium, sought to enter into rivalry with the celestial Gods, and, proud of their lofty origin, boasting an equal creation with these, revolted. Thus men became their instruments, opposed to one another, and fomenting civil wars. And thus, force oppressing weakness, the strong burnt and massacred the feeble, and quick and dead were thrust forth from the sacred places.

Then the elements resolved to complain before the Lord of the savage condition of mankind. For the evil being already very grievous, the elements hastened

[to

to God the Creator, and pleaded in this wise—the fire being suffered to speak first:—*

"O Master," he said, "Maker of this new world, Thou whose name, mysterious among the Gods, has hitherto been revered among all men; how long, O Divinity, hast Thou decreed to leave human life without God? Reveal Thyself to the world which calls for Thee, correct its savage existence by the institution of peace. Grant unto life, law, grant unto night oracles; fill all things with happy auguries; let

* In the Book of Enoch a similar legend appears—"The Giants turned themselves upon men to devour them, and began to do evil to birds and beasts of the field and reptiles and fish; and they devoured with one accord their flesh and drank their blood. When the earth lifted up her voice against the unjust, ... and because of the perdition of men, a cry arose that came even unto heaven. Therefore, Michael and Gabriel, and Souryan and Ouryan, looked forth from the height of heaven, and beheld the abundance of blood that was shed upon the earth, and all the iniquity that was accomplished, and they said one to another:—The voice of their cries ascends, the clamour of the earth is heard even at the gates of heaven, and before you, O holy ones of the skies, the souls of men complain, saying—Avenge us in the presence of the Lord. (VII. 14, 15; VIII. 8, 9; IX. 1, 2, 3.)

[See also the first book of Ovid's Metamorphoses, V., VI., VII. In all these accounts it appears that mankind is inspired to wickedness and impiety by the Giants, who are, in Hermetic teaching, explained to be the lower mundane forces, or "fallen Angels." They are, probably, the first created "souls" mentioned in an early passage of the allegory, and are elsewhere spoken of as Demons. Almost all the poets, whether Hebrew, Hellenic, Hindu, Persian, Norse, or Christian, celebrate the revolt of the Giants against heaven. It is needless to remind the reader that all these sacred fables have an esoteric and individual application, related to the Microcosm within man, as well as to the Macrocosm or world without. The text is manifestly imperfect. A. K.]

[men

men fear the judgment of the Gods, and no man shall sin any more. Let crimes receive their just punishment, and men will abstain from unrighteousness. They will fear to violate oaths, and madness will have an end. Teach them gratitude for benefits, so shall I devote my flame to pure offerings and libations, and the altars shall yield Thee exhalations of sweet savours. For now I am polluted, O Master, because the impious temerity of men forces me to consume flesh. They will not suffer me to remain in my nature; they pervert and corrupt my purity!"

The air spoke in its turn:—"I am defiled by the effluvium of corpses, O Master; I am becoming pestilent and unwholesome, and from on high I witness things which I ought not to behold."

Then the water took up the word, and spoke on this wise, O my illustrious son:—

"Father and wondrous Creator of all things, Divinity incarnate, Author of Nature who brings forth all through Thee, command the waters of the streams to be always pure, for now both rivers and seas are compelled to bathe the destroyer and to receive his victims!"

Then at the last the earth appeared, O my glorious son, and thus began:—

"O King, Chief of celestial choirs and Lord of their orbits, Master and Father of the elements which lend to all things increase and decrease, and into which all must return; behold how the impious and insensate tribe of man overspreads me, O venerable One, since by Thy commands I am the habitation of all beings, bearing them all and receiving into my bosom all that is slain; such is now my reproach. Thy terrestrial world in which all creatures are contained

[is bereft

is bereft of God. And because they revere nothing, they transgress every law and overwhelm me with all manner of evil works. To my shame, O Lord, I admit into myself the product of the corruption of carcases. But I, who receive all things, would fain also receive God. Grant to earth this grace, and if Thou comest not Thyself—for indeed I cannot contain Thee—let me at least receive some holy efflux of Thee. Let the earth become the most glorious of all the elements; and since she alone gives all things to all, may she revere herself as the recipient of Thy favours."

Thus the elements discoursed, and forthwith God filled the universe with His divine voice. "Go," said He, "sacred offspring, worthy of your Father's greatness, seek not to change anything, nor refuse to my creatures your ministry. I will send you an efflux of myself, a pure Being who shall investigate all actions, who shall be the dreadful and incorruptible Judge of the living; and sovereign justice shall extend its reign even into the shades beneath the earth. Thus shall every man receive his merited deserts."

Thereupon the elements ceased from their complaints, and each of them resumed its functions and its sway.

And in what manner, O my mother, said Horos, did the earth afterwards obtain this efflux of God?

I will not recount this Nativity, said Isis; I dare not, O powerful Horos, declare the origin of thy race, lest men in the future should learn the generation of the Gods. I will say only that the Supreme God, Creator and Architect of the world, at length accorded to earth for a season, thy father Osiris and the great Goddess Isis, that they might bring the expected

[salvation.

salvation. By them life attained its fulness; savage and bloody wars were ended; they consecrated temples to the Gods their ancestors, and instituted oblations. They gave to mortals law, nourishment, and raiment. "They shall read," Hermes said, "my mystic writings, and dividing them into two parts, they shall keep certain of them, and inscribe upon columns and obelisks those which may be useful to man." Institutors of the first tribunals, they established everywhere the reign of order and justice. With them began the faith of treaties, and the introduction into human life of the religious duty of oaths. They taught the rites of sepulture towards those who cease to live; they interrogated the horrors of death; they shewed that the spirit from without delights to return into the human body, and that if the way of entry be shut against it, it brings about a failure of life. Instructed by Hermes, they engraved upon hidden tables that the air is filled with genii. Instructed by Hermes in the secret laws of God, they alone were the teachers and legislators of mankind, initiating them in the arts, the sciences, and the benefits of civilised life. Instructed by Hermes concerning the sympathetic affinities which the Creator has established between heaven and earth, they instituted religious representations and sacred mysteries. And, considering the corruptible nature of all bodies, they ordained prophetic initiation, so that the prophet who lifts his hands to the Gods should be instructed in all things, and that thereby philosophy and magic might provide nourishment for the soul, and medicine might heal the sufferings of the flesh.

Having performed all these things, O my son, and seeing the world arrived at its fulness, Osiris and I were recalled by the inhabitants of heaven; but we

[could

could not return thither without having first praised the Lord, so that the celestial Vision might fill the expanse, and that the way of a happy ascension might open before us, since God delights in hymns.

O my mother, said Horos, teach me this hymn, that I also may be instructed in it.

Hearken, my son, answered Isis. . . .

PART II.

*   *   *   *

O MY illustrious son, if thou wilt know anything further, ask it of me. And Horos said, Revered Mother, I would fain know how royal souls are born. And Isis answered:—Herein, my son Horos, lies the distinctive character of royal souls. There are in the universe, four regions, governed by a fixed and immutable law: heaven, the ether, the air, and the most holy earth. Above, in heaven, dwell the Gods, ruled as are all the rest, by the Maker of the universe; in the ether are the stars, governed by the great fire, the sun; in the air are the souls of the genii, governed by the moon; upon earth are men and other animals governed by the soul who, for the time, is their king. For the Gods themselves engender those who shall be kings befitting the terrestrial race. Princes are the issue of kings, and he who is most kingly, is a greater

[king

king than the rest.* The sun, nearer to God than is the moon, is greater and stronger than she, and to him she is subject as much by rank as by power. The king is the last of the Gods and the first of men. So long as he sojourns upon earth, his divinity is concealed, but he possesses something which distinguishes him from other men and approximates him to God. The soul in him comes from a loftier region than that from which descend the souls of common men. Souls destined to reign upon the earth descend thither for two causes. There are those who in former lives have lived blameless, and who merit apotheosis: for such as these royalty is a preparation for the divine state. Again, there are holy souls who, for some slight infringement of the interior and divine law, receive in royalty a penance whereby the suffering and shame of incarnation are mitigated. The condition of these in taking a body resembles not that of others; they are as blessed as when they were free. †

As to the various characters of these kings, the variety is not in the souls, for all are royal, but it is due to the nature of the angels and genii who assist them. For souls destined to such offices are not without ministers and escort. Heavenly justice, even while exiling them from the abodes of the Blessed, treats them as their nature befits. When, then, O my son Horos, the ministering angels and genii appointed are warlike, the soul in their charge takes that character,

* This must not be understood in a vulgar sense of mere earthly monarchy, but of souls whose destiny it is to be chiefs and leaders among men, whether spiritually, intellectually, or politically.

A. K.

† This passage perhaps refers, though obscurely, to Avâtars of souls who have already attained beatitude, though not apotheosis.

A. K.

[forgetting

forgetting its own, or rather laying it aside until some future change of condition. If the guardian angels are of a gentle order, then the soul follows its path in peace; if they are friends of judgment, the soul loves to judge; if they are musicians, then the soul sings; if they love truth, the soul is that of a philosopher. Thus the souls necessarily follow the teaching of their guardians; falling into human bodies they forego their proper estate, and while exiled from it they approximate to those intelligences by whom they have been embodied.

Thine explanation is complete, my mother, said Horos, but thou hast not yet informed me in what manner noble souls are born.

There are upon earth, O my son, different offices. So also is it among souls; they occupy different stations, and that soul which issues from a more exalted sphere is nobler than the rest; even as he who is free among men, is nobler than the slave. Exalted and royal souls are necessarily the masters of men.

How are souls born male or female?

Souls, my son Horos, are all equal in nature, since they come from one region wherein the Creator has formed them. There are not among them either males or females; this distinction exists only between bodies, and not between incorporeal beings. But some are more energetic, some are gentler; and this belongs to the air in which all things are formed. For an airy body envelopes the soul; in it are the elements of earth, water, air, and fire. Among females this combination contains more of cold and of moisture than of dryness and heat, and the soul which is enfolded therein is watery and disposed to softness. The contrary happens among males; their envelope contains

[more

more of dryness and of heat, less of cold and of moisture; hence in bodies so formed the souls manifest greater vivacity and energy.

And how, O my mother, are born the souls of the wise?

And Isis answered:—The organ of vision is enveloped in tunics. When these tunics are thick and dense, the sight is dull; when they are fine and subtle, the sight is penetrating. Even so is it with the soul; she likewise has her coverings, incorporeal as herself. These coverings are the interior airs; when they are subtle, clear, and transparent, then the soul is perspicuous; when, on the contrary, they are dense, thick, and turgid, then she cannot see far; and discerns only, as though in cloudy weather, that which lies immediately before her steps.

And Horos said:—For what reason, my mother, are the minds of men who are not of our holy country less open than the minds of those who belong to it?

And Isis replied *:—The earth is set in the midst of the universe like a man lying on his back and gazing into heaven, and the various regions of earth correspond to the different members of the man. The earth turns her gaze towards heaven as towards her father, following in her changes the changes of the skies. Her head lies to the south, her right shoulder to the east, her left is turned towards the Lybian wind, her feet are under the constellation of the Bear, the right beneath the tail, and the left beneath the head

---

* I believe the whole of the ensuing passage to be highly metaphorical, and to relate to the occult distinctions and divisions of the seven great races of mankind. It is not difficult to interpret the allusions. A. K.

[of the

of the Bear; her loins are under the regions of heaven nearest to the Bear; the midst of her body is beneath the centre of heaven. Behold as a proof of these things, how they who dwell in the South have a beautiful countenance and plentiful hair, while the orientals have hands hardy in conflict and ready with the bow, for they are right-handed; the westerns are strong and fight with the left hand, attributing to the left side the functions which belong in others to the right; those who dwell beneath the Bear are distinguished by the attributes of their feet, and by the beauty of their legs; those who inhabit beyond the Bear in the climate of Italy and of Greece are remarkable for the beauty of their loins, and hence their tendency to prefer males. This part of the body also, being whiter than the rest, produces men of a whiter hue. The hallowed region of our ancestors is in the midst of the earth, and since the midst of the human body is the seat of the heart, and the heart of the soul, this is why, my son, the men of this land, beside the qualities which all men possess in common, have also a loftier intelligence and wisdom, because the heart of the earth brings them forth and nourishes them.

Moreover, my son, the south is the storehouse of the clouds; it is there they assemble, and thence, it is said, flows our river (Nile), when the cold becomes abundant. Now, where the clouds descend, the air grows thick and is filled with vapours which spread themselves as a veil not only over the sight, but over the intelligence. The east, my son Horos, is continually disturbed and glowing under the sunrise, as is the west under the sunset; therefore, they who dwell in these regions can hardly preserve a clear perception. The north, by means of its icy temperature, thickens the mind even as it does the body.

[The

The central land alone, clear and serene, is favoured as are those who inhabit her. She brings forth in a perpetual tranquillity, she adorns and completes her offspring, she contends alone against all others, she triumphs, and like a worthy ruler partakes with the vanquished the fruits of victory.

Explain to me further, my august Mother, what it is that causes in living men during long maladies, an alteration of discernment, of reason, even of the soul itself.

And Isis answered:—Among animals there are those who have affinity with fire, others with water, others with earth, others with air, others again with two or three elements, or with all the four. Or, inversely, some have an antipathy for fire, some for water, some for earth, some for air, or again for two, three or four elements. Thus, the locust and all kinds of insects flee from the fire; the eagle, the hawk, and other birds of flight fear the water; the fish dread the air and earth; the serpent abhors the open air, and like all crawling creatures loves the ground; all fishes delight in the deep, the birds in the air where they pass their lives; those who fly highest delight in the fire (of the sun) and sojourn in its vicinity. There are even certain creatures who disport themselves in the fire, such are the salamanders who have their abode in it. The elements enfold the body, and every soul inhabiting a body is weighed down and enchained by the four elements; wherefore, it is natural that the soul should have affinity with certain elements and aversion for others, for which reason she cannot enjoy perfect happiness. Nevertheless, as the soul is of divine origin, she struggles and meditates even beneath this bodily covering; but her thoughts are not what they would be if she were free from the body. And

[if the

if the body be disturbed and troubled by sickness or by terror, the soul herself is tossed about like a man in the midst of tempestuous waves.

   * * * *

PART III.

*   *   *   *

THOU hast given me admirable instruction, O my most powerful Mother Isis, concerning the marvellous creation of Souls by God, and I am filled with wonder; but thou hast not yet shewn me whither souls depart when set free from bodies. Fain would I contemplate this mystery, and thank only thee for the initiation.

And Isis said :—Hearken, my son, for thy most necessary enquiry holds an important place, and may not be neglected. Hear my reply.

O great and marvellous scion of the illustrious Osiris, think not that souls on quitting the body mix themselves confusedly in the vague immensity and become dispersed in the universal and infinite spirit, without power to return into bodies, to preserve their identity, or to seek again their primeval abode. Water spilt from a vase returns no more to its place therein, it has no proper locality, it mingles itself with the mass of waters; but it is not thus with souls, O most wise Horos. I am

[initiated

initiated into the mysteries of the immortal nature; I walk in the ways of the truth, and I will reveal all to thee without the least omission. And first I will tell thee that water, being a body without reason, composed of myriads of fluid particles, differs from the soul which is, my son, a personal entity, the royal work of the hands and of the mind of God, abiding herself in intelligence. That which proceeds from Unity, and not from multiplicity, cannot mingle with other things, and in order that the soul may be joined to the body, God subjects this harmonious union to Necessity.

Souls do not, then, return confusedly, nor by chance, into one and the same place, but each is despatched into the condition which belongs to her. And this is determined by that which the soul experiences while yet she is in the tenement of the body, loaded with a burden contrary to her nature. Hear: therefore, this comparison, O beloved Horos; suppose that there should be shut up in the same prison, men, eagles, doves, swans, hawks, swallows, sparrows, flies, serpents, lions, leopards, wolves, dogs, hares, oxen, sheep, and certain amphibious animals, such as seals, hydras, turtles, crocodiles, and that at the same moment all the creatures should be liberated. All at once would escape; the men would seek cities and the public places, the eagles the ether, where nature teaches them to live, the doves the lower air, the hawks the higher expanse; the swallows would repair to places frequented by men, the sparrows to the orchards, the swans to districts where they could sing; the flies would haunt the proximity of the ground as high only as human exhalations extend, for the property of flies is to live on these and to flit over the surface of the earth; the lions and leopards would flee to the mountains, the wolves to the solitudes; the dogs would follow the track of man;

[the

the hares would betake themselves to the woods, the oxen to the fields and meadows, the sheep to the pastures; the serpents would seek the caves of the earth; the seals and the turtles would rejoin their kind in the shallows and running waters, in order to enjoy, conformably to their nature, alike the proximity of the shore and of the deep. Each creature would return, conducted by its own interior discernment, into the abode befitting it. Even so every soul, whether human or inhabiting the earth under other conditions, knows whither she ought to go; unless, indeed, some son of Typhon should pretend that a bull may subsist in the waters or a turtle in the air. If, then, even when immersed in flesh and blood, souls do not infringe the law of order, although under penance,—for union with the body is a penance,—how much more shall they conform thereto when delivered from their bonds and set at liberty!

Now this most holy law, which extends even unto heaven, is on this wise, O illustrious child: behold the hierarchy of souls! The expanse between the empyrean and the moon is occupied by the Gods, the stars, and the powers of providence. Between the moon and ourselves, my son, is the abode of the souls. The unmeasured air, which we call the wind, has in itself an appointed way in which it moves to refresh the earth, as I shall by and by relate. But this movement of the air upon itself impedes not the way of the souls, nor does it hinder them from ascending and descending without obstacle; they flow across the air without mingling in it, or confounding themselves therewith, as water flows over oil. This expanse, my son, is divided into four provinces, and into sixty regions. The first province from the earth upwards comprehends four regions, and extends as far as certain summits or promontories, which

[it is

it is unable to transcend. The second province comprises eight regions in which the motions of the winds arise. Be thou attentive, my son, for thou hearest the ineffable mysteries of the earth, the heavens, and of the sacred fluid which lies between.* In the province of the winds fly the birds; above this there is no moving air nor any creature. But the air with all the beings it contains distributes itself into all boundaries within its reach, and into the four quarters of the earth, while the earth cannot lift itself into the mansions of the air. The third province comprehends sixteen regions filled with a pure and subtle element. The fourth contains thirty-two regions, in which the air, wholly subtle and diaphanous, allows itself to be penetrated by the element of fire. Such is the order which, without confusion, reigns from depth to height;—to wit, four general divisions, twelve intervals, sixty regions, and in these dwell the souls, each according to the nature thereof. They are indeed all of one substance, but they constitute a hierarchy; and the further any region is removed from the earth, the loftier is the dignity of the souls which dwell therein.

And now it remains to be explained to thee, O most glorious Horos, what souls they are who abide in each of these regions, and this I shall set forth, beginning by the most exalted.

The expanse which stretches between earth and heaven is divided into regions, my son Horos, according to measure and harmony. To these regions our ancestors have given various names; some call them

* This hint is enough to indicate that Isis speaks in metaphorical language. The entire description should be understood as equally applicable to the macrocosm and the microcosm, the consciousness of every constituent particle in man's system being accounted a soul.
A. K.

zones, others firmaments, others spheres. Therein dwell the souls who are freed from bodies, and those who have not yet been incorporated. The stations which they occupy correspond with their dignity. In the upper region are the divine and royal souls; the baser souls—they who float over the surface of the earth—are in the lowest sphere, and in the middle regions are the souls of ordinary degree. Thus, my son, the souls destined to rule descend from the superior zones, and when they are delivered from the body, thither they return, or even higher still, unless indeed they have acted contrary to the dignity of their nature and to the laws of God. For, if they have transgressed, the Providence on high causes them to descend into the lower regions according to the measure of their faults; and in like manner also it conducts other souls, inferior in power and dignity, from the lower spheres into a more exalted abode. For on high dwell two ministers of the universal Providence; one is guardian of the souls, the other is their conductor, who sends them forth and ordains for them bodies. The first minister guards them, the second releases or binds them, according to the will of God.

In this wise the law of equity presides over the changes which take place above, even as upon earth also it moulds and constructs the vessels in which the souls are immured. This law is supplemented by two energies, Memory and Experience. Memory directs in Nature the preservation and maintenance of all the original types appointed in heaven; the function of Experience s to provide every soul descending into generation with a body appropriate thereto; so that passionate souls should have vigorous bodies; slothful souls sluggard bodies; active souls active bodies; gentle souls gentle bodies; powerful souls powerful bodies; cunning

[souls

souls dexterous bodies;—briefly, that every soul should have a befitting nature. For it is not without just cause that winged creatures are clothed with feathers; that intelligent creatures are gifted with finer senses and superior to others; that beasts of the field are furnished with horns, with tusks, with claws, or other weapons; that reptiles are endowed with undulating and flexible bodies, and lest the moisture of their natures should render them feeble, are armed either with teeth or with pointed scales, so that they are, even less than others, in peril of death. As for fishes, these timid souls have allotted to them for a dwelling-place that element in which light is bereft of its double activity, for in the water, fire neither illuminates nor burns. Each fish, swimming by the help of his spiny fins, flies where he wills, and his weakness is protected by the obscurity of the deep. Thus are souls immured in bodies resembling themselves; in human shape, those souls who have received reason; in flying creatures, souls of a wild nature; in beasts, souls without reason, whose only law is force; in reptiles, deceitful souls, for they attack not their prey face to face, but by ambush; while fishes enshrine those timid souls who merit not the enjoyment of other elements.

In every order of animals there are individuals who transgress the laws of their being.

In what way, my Mother? said Horos.

And Isis answered: In this wise:—A man who acts against reason, a beast which eludes necessity, a reptile which forgets its cunning, a fish which loses its timidity, a bird which renounces freedom. Thou hast heard what was to be said concerning the hierarchy of souls, their descent, and the creation of bodies.

O my son, in every order of souls there are found a

[few

few royal souls, and of divers characters: some fiery, some cold, some proud, some gentle, some crafty, some simple, some contemplative, some active. This diversity belongs to the regions from whence they descend into bodies. From the royal zone the royal souls go forth, but there are many royalties; the royalty of spirit, of the flesh, of art, of science, of the virtues.

And how, said Horos, dost thou name these royalties?

O my son, the king of souls who have hitherto existed is thy father Osiris; the king of bodies is the prince of each nation, he who governs. The king of wisdom is the Father of all things; the Initiator is the thrice great Hermes; over medicine presides Asclepios, the son of Hephaistos; force and power are under the sway of Osiris, and after him, under thine, my son. Philosophy depends on Arnebaskenis; poetry, yet again, on Asclepios, Imouthè's son. So that, if thou thinkest thereon, thou wilt perceive that there are indeed many royalties and many kings.

But the supreme royalty belongs to the highest region; lesser kingships correspond to the spheres which bring them forth. Those who issue from the fiery zone handle fire; those who come from the watery zone frequent liquid spheres; from the region of art and learning those are born who devote themselves to art and science; from the region of inactivity, those who live in ease and idleness. All that is done and said upon earth has its origin in the heights, from whence all essences are dispensed with measure and equilibrium; nor is there anything which does not emanate from above and return thither.

Explain to me this that thou sayest, O my Mother.

[And

And Isis answered:—An evident token of these changes has been stamped on all creatures by most ly Nature. The breath which we indraw from the per air we exhale and again inbreathe by means of e lungs within us which perform this work. And en the way destined to receive our breath is closed, en no longer do we remain on earth; we depart hence. oreover, O my glorious son, there are other accidents which the balance of our combination may be stroyed.*

What is, then, this combination, O my Mother?

It is the union and admixture of the four elements, ence emanates a vapour which envelops the soul, netrates into the body and communicates to both its n character. Thus are produced varieties among uls and bodies. If in the composition of a body, fire minates, then the soul being already of an ardent ture, receives thereby an excess of heat which renders the more energetic and furious, and the body the re vivacious and active. If the air dominates, the dy and soul of the creature are thereby rendered stable, errant and restless. The domination of the ter causes the soul to be mild, affable, bland, sociable, d easily moulded, because water blends and mixes itself adily with all other things, dissolves them if it be undant, moistens and penetrates them if it be less in antity. A body softened by too much humidity offers t a weak resistance, a slight malady disintegrates it, d little by little dissolves its cohesion. Again, if the rthy element be dominant, the soul is obtuse, because e body lacks subtlety, nor can she force a way through e density of its organism. Therefore, the soul remains

* Isis here speaks not as a Goddess, but as a mortal.

A.K.

[indrawn

indrawn upon herself, borne down by the burden she supports, and the body is solid, inactive, and heavy, moving only with effort.

But if the elements be all in just equilibrium, then the whole nature is ardent in its actions, subtle in its motions, fluent in its sensations, and of a robust constitution. Of the predominance of air and fire birds are born, whose nature resembles that of the elements which generate them. Men are endowed with an abundance of fire united with but a little air, and of water and earth equal parts. This excess of fire becomes sagacity, seeing that intelligence is indeed a kind of flame, which consumes not, but which penetrates. The predominance of water and earth with a sufficient admixture of air and but little fire engenders beasts; those endued with more fire than the rest are the more courageous. Water and earth in equal quantities give birth to reptiles, which, being deprived of fire, have neither courage nor truthfulness, while the excess of water renders them cold, that of earth, sordid and heavy, and the lack of air makes all their movements difficult. Much water with but little earth produces fishes; the absence of fire and air in them causes their timidity, and disposes them to lie hidden, while the predominance of water and earth in their nature approximates them by natural affinity to earth dissolved in water. Moreover, by means of the proportional increase of the elements composing the body is the body itself increased, and its development ceases when the full measure is attained. And so long, my beloved son, as equilibrium is maintained in the primitive combination and in the vapours arising therefrom, that is, so long as the normal proportion of fire, air, earth, and water remains unchanged, the creature continues in

[health.

health. But if the elements deviate from the proportion originally determined—(I speak not now of the growth of activities, nor of that resulting from a change of order, but of a rupture of equilibrium whether by addition or diminution of fire or of other elements)—then malady supervenes. And should air and fire, whose nature is one with that of the soul itself, prevail in the conflict, then, through the dominance of those elements, destroyers of the flesh, the creature abandons its proper state. For the earthy element is the pabulum of the body, and the water wherewith it is permeated contributes to consolidate it; but it is the aerial element which confers motion, and the fire engenders all energies. The vapours produced by the union and combination of these elements blending with the soul, as it were by fusion, bear her along with them, and clothe her in their own nature, whether good or evil. So long as she remains in this natural association the soul keeps the rank she has attained. But if a change should occur either in the combination itself or in any of its parts or subdivisions, the vapours, altering their condition, alter likewise the relations between soul and body; the fire and air, aspiring upward, draw with them the soul, their sister, while the watery and terrestrial elements, which tend earthwards like the body, weigh it down and overwhelm it.

* * * *

End of the Virgin of the World.

This is the end of this publication.

Any remaining blank pages are for our book binding requirements and are blank on purpose.

To search thousands of interesting publications like this one, please remember to visit our website at:

http://www.kessinger.net

CPSIA information can be obtained
at www.ICGtesting.com
Printed in the USA
LVHW061352151121
703385LV00003B/325